I0824242

AMERICAN HOLIDAYS AND CELEBRATIONS

CHRISTMAS

Jessica Coupé

LIGHTBOX
openlightbox.com

Go to **www.openlightbox.com** and enter this book's unique code.

ACCESS CODE

LBXL7728

Lightbox is an all-inclusive digital solution for the teaching and learning of curriculum topics in an original, groundbreaking way. Lightbox is based on National Curriculum Standards.

LIGHTBOX SUPPLEMENTARY RESOURCES

SHARE
Share titles within your Learning Management System (LMS) or Library Circulation System

CURRICULUM
Find national and state curriculum correlations

CITATION
Create bibliographical references following APA, CMOS, and MLA styles

STANDARD FEATURES OF LIGHTBOX

AUDIO High-quality narration using text-to-speech system

ACTIVITIES Printable PDFs that can be emailed and graded

SLIDESHOWS Pictorial overviews of key concepts

VIDEOS Embedded high-definition video clips

WEBLINKS Curated links to external, child-safe resources

TRANSPARENCIES Step-by-step layering of maps, diagrams, charts, and timelines

INTERACTIVE MAPS Interactive maps and aerial satellite imagery

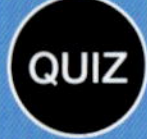
QUIZZES Ten multiple-choice questions that are automatically graded and emailed for teacher assessment

KEY WORDS Matching key concepts to their definitions

This title is part of our Lightbox digital subscription

Lightbox Grades 3–5 Subscription
ISBN 978-1-5105-5424-5

Access hundreds of Lightbox titles with our digital subscription. Sign up for a **FREE** subscription trial at **www.openlightbox.com/trial**

The digital components of this book are guaranteed to stay active for at least five years from the date of publication.

CHRISTMAS

CONTENTS

2 Lightbox Access Code
4 What Is Christmas?
6 Christmas History
8 Important People
10 Christmas Celebrations
12 Celebrating Today
14 Christmas in the United States
16 Christmas Symbols
18 Christmas Stories
19 Write Your Own Story
20 Make a Christmas Snow Globe
21 Candy Cane Christmas Cookies
22 Christmas Quiz
23 Key Words/Index

What Is Christmas?

Every year, on December 25, many Americans celebrate Christmas. Settlers brought this holiday to America more than 200 years ago. Christmas celebrates the birth of Jesus Christ, a man who **Christians** believe was the son of God. Christmas is a time for Christians to remember the story of Jesus's birth.

Christmas is no longer a holiday just for Christians, however. Over time, it has become a day that anyone can celebrate. The Christmas season is known as a festive time. People across the country decorate their homes with lights and ornaments. They exchange gifts with friends and loved ones.

Communities often stage Nativity plays during the Christmas season. These plays tell the story of Jesus's birth.

Christmas History

No one knows the exact date of Jesus's birth. It was never recorded in the **Bible**. In the 4th century AD, the **Roman Catholic** Church made an important decision. It decided that Jesus's birthday would always be celebrated on December 25. This date was chosen because December was already a festive time of year. For many years, the **Romans** had held a festival called Saturnalia in December.

Timeline

5th century BC

The people of ancient Rome begin holding their festival of Saturnalia every December to honor the god Saturn.

4th century AD

Pope Julius I, the leader of the Roman Catholic Church, declares that Jesus's birthday will be commemorated on December 25 every year. Known as the Feast of the Nativity, the holiday slowly spreads, reaching England by the end of the 6th century.

1644

A group known as the Puritans bans Christmas in England, believing that its religious significance has been lost. Puritan settlers in America also refuse to acknowledge the holiday.

During Saturnalia, the Romans lit candles as a **symbol** of Saturn's light. They would place these candles on trees. Christians began following this **tradition** as well. They placed a candle on a tree as a symbol of the star that led people to the place where Jesus was born.

On Christmas Eve, many churches hold candlelight services. The candles are said to represent the light of Jesus Christ coming into the world.

As time passed, people all over the world began to celebrate Christmas. They mixed Christian traditions with those from other winter festivals. When European settlers moved to the United States, they continued to celebrate their Christmas traditions.

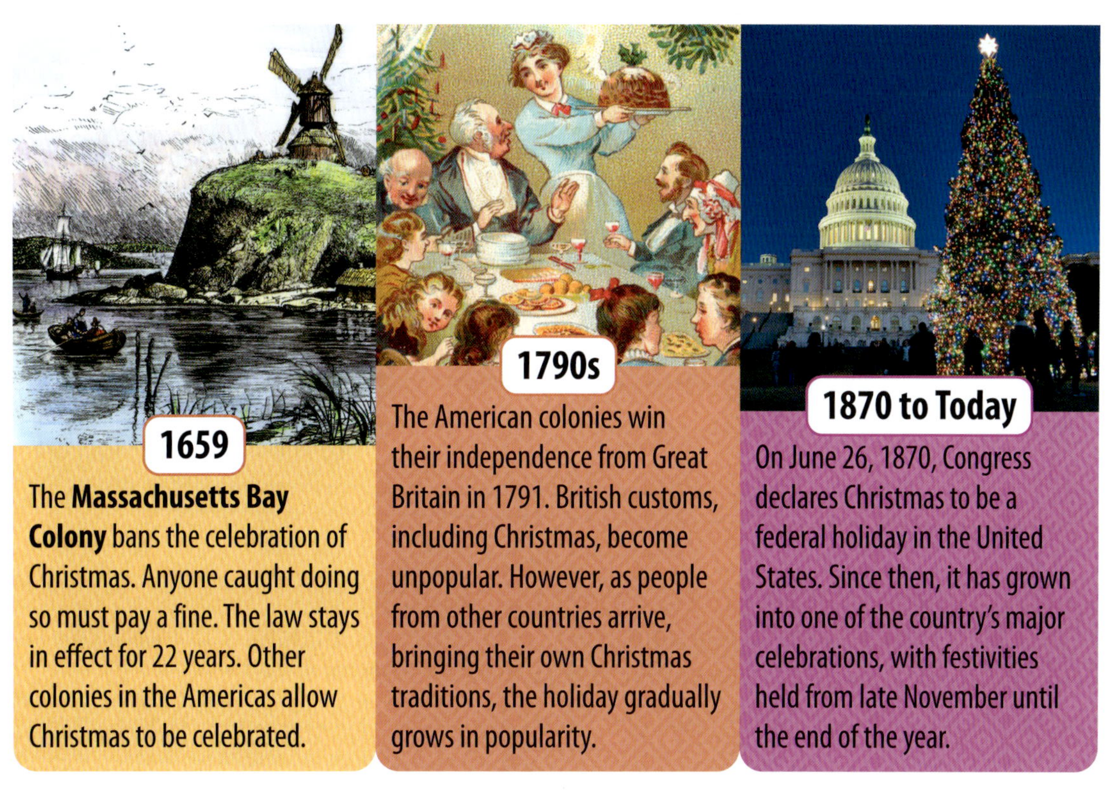

1659

The **Massachusetts Bay Colony** bans the celebration of Christmas. Anyone caught doing so must pay a fine. The law stays in effect for 22 years. Other colonies in the Americas allow Christmas to be celebrated.

1790s

The American colonies win their independence from Great Britain in 1791. British customs, including Christmas, become unpopular. However, as people from other countries arrive, bringing their own Christmas traditions, the holiday gradually grows in popularity.

1870 to Today

On June 26, 1870, Congress declares Christmas to be a federal holiday in the United States. Since then, it has grown into one of the country's major celebrations, with festivities held from late November until the end of the year.

Important People

Christians have celebrated the birth of Jesus Christ for almost 2,000 years. The story of his birth begins with a woman named Mary, who lived in the city of Nazareth. One night, an angel visited Mary and told her that she had been chosen to be the mother of God's son.

Shortly after the angel's visit, Mary married a man named Joseph. As the time for the baby's birth drew near, Joseph took Mary to the town of Bethlehem. When they arrived, all of the inns were full. A kind innkeeper let Mary and Joseph stay in his stable. That night, Mary gave birth to Jesus.

Jesus grew up to become a teacher and religious leader. He taught people how to live a spiritual life and how to treat others. Many believed in his teachings. They became his followers, helping to establish the Christian religion. Christianity continues to flourish to this day, with an estimated 2.4 billion followers worldwide.

MAJOR WORLD RELIGIONS

	Christianity	Islam	Hinduism	Buddhism	Judaism
Symbol					
Followers Worldwide	2.4 billion	2 billion	1.2 billion	507 million	14.6 million
Name of Deity	God	Allah	Brahma, Vishnu, Shiva	No deity	Yahweh
Principle Figure	Jesus Christ	Muhammad	No one founder	Buddha	Abraham
Sacred Texts	Bible	Qu'ran	No one book	No one book	Hebrew Bible

Bethlehem continues to honor its links to Jesus's birth. During the Christmas season, its main square becomes the center of Christmas activities, including Nativity scenes, parades, and a midnight mass church service.

Christmas Celebrations

In the early days of American settlement, those who celebrated Christmas did so with traditions from their home countries. English settlers would decorate their houses with holly, ivy, and mistletoe. They would stroll the streets, singing popular English Christmas **carols**. On Christmas Day, they attended church services, held parties, put on plays, and feasted.

German settlers brought the tradition of the Christmas tree to their new American home. They also introduced **advent** calendars. People would use the calendar to count down to Christmas day. Every day starting on December 1, they would open a door in the calendar and take out a small gift. German and other European settlers also saw Christmas as a time to bake goodies and give gifts.

The children of both English and Dutch settlers looked forward to a special visitor at Christmastime. While English children waited for Father Christmas, Dutch children watched out for Saint Nicholas. Writers created stories and poems about these legendary figures. Over the years, they became known as a man called Santa Claus.

Unlike the Santa Claus of today, Father Christmas did not always wear a red suit. Many early pictures had him dressed in a brown suit.

Celebrations Around the World

China

China's Dongzhi Festival has been held every December since at least 206 BC. It takes place during the **winter solstice** and celebrates winter's arrival. The Dongzhi Festival is a time for people to worship heaven and hope that they will have good health and a good harvest.

Israel

Celebrated by Jewish people around the world, Hanukkah is a national holiday in Israel. Lasting eight days starting in November or December, Hanukkah remembers the re-dedication of a Jewish temple following a battle. People celebrate by lighting candles. It is a time of pride in Israel.

Sweden

On December 13, Sweden celebrates St. Lucia Day. St. Lucia was known for taking food to the needy. She would wear candles on her head to light the way. To honor St. Lucia, young women across Sweden take part in processions and ceremonies, many dressed as the saint.

Celebrating Today

Today, families across the nation decorate their Christmas tree and add Christmas lights to the outside of their house. Some put ornaments on their lawn. Children write to Santa Claus, telling him what they want for Christmas. People send greeting cards to loved ones. The smell of Christmas baking wafts through many homes.

Christmas is family time. Families may sit down to watch Christmas movies or read holiday stories to each other. Some get together to go skating or sledding. Others take sleigh rides across the countryside. On Christmas Day, families often gather for big dinners.

Turkey is a staple food in a traditional Christmas dinner. Side dishes can include stuffing, mashed potatoes, gravy, green beans, and cranberry sauce, with a pie or Yule log cake for dessert.

People also celebrate Christmas with their community. They may attend church services, Nativity plays, or Christmas parties. Many communities have parades and tree-lighting ceremonies for people to enjoy. People often help others at Christmas. They give food, toys, or clothing to those who cannot afford them.

Giving back to the community is an important way to mark the holiday season. It is estimated that volunteerism increases by about 50 percent at this time of year.

WHAT AMERICA EATS AT CHRISTMAS

7.3 billion Shrimp

1.58 billion Candy canes

22 million Turkeys

Christmas in the United States

Approximately 90 percent of Americans celebrate Christmas. Communities across the country stage a variety of festivities over the holiday season. This map shows a few of the Christmas events that take place in November and December.

A California
San Diego
100,000 people attend each year

B Texas
Houston
400,000 people attend each year

C Minnesota
St. Paul
188,000 people attend each year

D Illinois
Chicago
800,000 people attend each year

E New York
New York City
2 million people attend each year

A San Diego

San Diego, California, has been holding its Parade of Lights for more than 50 years. Every December, the city's waters come alive as more than 80 boats parade through the harbor, each lavishly decorated to match the year's theme.

B Houston

One of the most popular Christmas events in Houston, Texas, is the Zoo Lights festival. Held at the Houston Zoo, this evening event allows visitors to sip on hot chocolate as they walk through light displays that are made to look like animals and plants.

C St. Paul

CHS Field, a sports arena in St. Paul, Minnesota, becomes awash with light over the Christmas season with the city's Glow Holiday Festival. This walk-through event uses more than 1 million Christmas lights to create festive scenes and scenery.

D Chicago

For more than 30 years, the Christmas season in Chicago, Illinois, has started in November with the city's Magnificent Mile Lights Festival. This event includes a tree-lighting ceremony, parade, and fireworks display.

E New York City

New York City's Radio City Music Hall has been hosting its Christmas Spectacular since 1933. Starring the Rockettes precision dance troupe, the show also features live music, video projections, and a guest appearance by Santa Claus.

Christmas Symbols

When people think about Christmas, certain items come to mind. As each represents the holiday in some way, it is known as a symbol of the season. Symbols often serve to remind people of the story behind a holiday.

Christmas Stars

When decorating their Christmas tree, many people place a star at its very top. Stars are also a popular shape for Christmas cookies, crafts, and decorations. The reason for this is that a star is linked to the story of Jesus's birth. Shortly after Jesus was born, three wise men came to visit him. They were led to the stable in Bethlehem by a star shining brightly in the night sky.

The star is often the last Christmas ornament to be put on the tree. It is considered to be the finishing touch.

Gifts

Giving gifts is a key part of today's Christmas celebrations. Gifts are put under Christmas trees and exchanged at parties. The tradition of gift-giving also has its roots in the story of Jesus's birth. When the three wise men visited Jesus, they each presented him with a gift. The Christmas gifts people give today honor those that the wise men gave Jesus long ago.

Candy Canes

Candy canes are among the best-known Christmas treats. They were first made in the late 17th century. Traditionally, candy canes were a red-and-white striped candy, but they now come in many colors and flavors. A candy cane is shaped like a shepherd's crook. This shape reminds people that Jesus is a good shepherd who leads his flock to peace and safety.

Outdoor Christmas displays often feature decorations that look like candy canes.

Christmas Stories

Stories are an important part of Christmas. There are many stories about Santa Claus, his elves, and his reindeer. An early Christmas story was *A Visit from Saint Nicholas*, written by Clement Clarke Moore more than 200 years ago. Here is a part of that story.

'Twas the night before Christmas, when all through the house
Not a creature was stirring, not even a mouse;
The stockings were hung by the chimney with care,
In hopes that St. Nicholas soon would be there;

The children were nestled all snug in their beds,
While visions of sugar-plums danced in their heads;
And Mama in her kerchief, and I in my cap,
Had just settled our brains for a long winter's nap;

When out on the lawn there arose such a clatter,
I sprang from the bed to see what was the matter.
Away to the window I flew like a flash,
Tore open the shutters and threw up the sash.

The moon on the breast of the new-fallen snow,
Gave the lustre of midday to objects below,
When, what to my wondering sight should appear,
But a miniature sleigh, and eight tiny reindeer,

With a little old driver, so lively and quick,
I knew in a moment it must be St. Nick.

Write Your Own Story

Writing a Christmas story is a fun way to enjoy the festive season. You can write your own story by following the steps below.

1

Brainstorm ideas for your story. What type of tale do you want to write? Will it be a Christmas adventure, a mystery, or something else? Choose an idea that really interests you.

2

Create a main character for your Christmas story. It might feature a reindeer, snowman, or a tiny elf. Whatever you choose, give your character a name.

3

Develop a **plot** for your story. Think about a problem this character might face at Christmastime. Determine the steps your character might take to solve it.

4

Write your story. Include what the main character says, sees, hears, and smells. These details will help your readers see the story in their minds.

5

Share your story with friends. Your story might start a new Christmas tradition!

TIP

People sometimes look to other Christmas stories to find inspiration for their own. Try reading books and watching movies about Christmas to get ideas for your story.

Make a Christmas Snow Globe

Snow globes have been a popular Christmas ornament since the 1940s. People shake the snow globe to watch the snow inside it fall.

Materials Needed

Directions

1. Place a dab of glue on the inside of the jar lid. Attach the plastic figurine to it.
2. Fill the jar with distilled water. This water will not cloud up as easily as tap water.
3. Add 1 to 2 teaspoons (5 to 10 milliliters) of glitter and stir. Screw the base or lid onto the jar.
4. Apply glue around the lid to help prevent leaks. Let the glue dry.
5. Shake your snow globe and watch it snow.

Candy Cane Christmas Cookies

Ingredients Needed

1½ cups (355 mL) all-purpose flour
1 teaspoon (5 mL) baking powder
½ teaspoon (2.5 mL) baking soda
¼ teaspoon (1.2 mL) salt
½ cup (120 mL) unsalted butter, softened
½ cup (120 mL) granulated sugar
1/3 cup (80 mL) brown sugar
1 large egg
2 teaspoons (10 mL) vanilla extract
Crushed candy cane

Materials Needed

Parchment paper
2 Bowls
2 cookie sheets
Whisk
Teaspoon
Cooling racks
Hand mixer
Rolling pin

Directions

1. With an adult's help, preheat oven to 350° Fahrenheit (175° Celsius). Line cookie sheets with parchment paper.
2. In a bowl, whisk the flour, baking powder, baking soda, and salt together. Set aside.
3. In a separate bowl, beat the butter and both sugars with the hand mixer until light and fluffy. Whip in the egg and vanilla extract until combined.
4. Add the flour mixture to the wet ingredients with the mixer set at low speed.
5. Crush the candy canes with a rolling pin. Stir the candy into the dough.
6. Scoop balls of dough onto the baking sheets, leaving 1 or 2 inches (2.5 to 5 centimeters) between each ball.
7. Bake for 8 to 11 minutes. Remove the cookies from the oven when they are firm on the bottom.
8. Let the cookies cool on the cooling racks. Once cool, eat and enjoy.

Christmas Quiz

ANSWERS: 1. Almost 2,000 years 2. June 26, 1870 3. A play that tells the story of Jesus's birth 4. December 13 5. Saturnalia 6. 90 percent 7. 1659 8. The Christmas tree and advent calendar 9. Late 17th century 10. 2.4 billion

Key Words

advent: the period that begins four Sundays before Christmas, during which Christians prepare for the holiday with prayer and fasting

Bible: a collection of religious texts that are held to be sacred in Christianity

carols: songs or hymns about Christmas

Christians: people who follow the teachings of Jesus Christ

Massachusetts Bay Colony: one of the original English settlements in the present-day state of Massachusetts

plot: the main events of a story

Roman Catholic: relating to the Christian church that has the Pope of Rome as its leader

Romans: an ancient people who ruled much of Britain, Europe, and the Middle East for thousands of years

symbol: a sign, shape, or object that is used to represent something else

tradition: a behavior or belief that has been established for a long time

winter solstice: the shortest day and longest night of the year

Index

advent calendars 10

Bethlehem 8, 9, 16

candy canes 13, 17, 21, 22
Christian 5, 7, 8, 22
Christmas carols 10
Christmas lights 5, 12, 15
Christmas stars 16
Christmas tree 7, 10, 12, 13, 15, 16, 17, 22

Dongzhi Festival 11

Father Christmas 10
food 11, 12, 13

gifts 5, 10, 17
greeting cards 12

Hanukkah 11

Jesus Christ 5, 6, 7, 8, 9, 16, 17, 22
Joseph 8

Mary 8
Massachusetts Bay Colony 7, 22
Moore, Clement Clarke 18

Nativity plays 5, 12, 13, 22

ornaments 5, 12, 16, 20

parades 9, 13, 15
Pope Julius I 6
Puritans 6

Romans 6, 7, 22

Saint Nicholas 10, 18
Santa Claus 10, 12, 15, 18
Saturnalia 6, 7, 22
settlers 5, 6, 7, 10, 22
St. Lucia Day 11, 22

LIGHTBOX

SUPPLEMENTARY RESOURCES

Click on the plus icon found in the bottom left corner of each spread to open additional teacher resources.

- Download and print the book's quizzes and activities
- Access curriculum correlations
- Explore additional web applications that enhance the Lightbox experience

LIGHTBOX DIGITAL TITLES
Packed full of integrated media

VIDEOS

INTERACTIVE MAPS

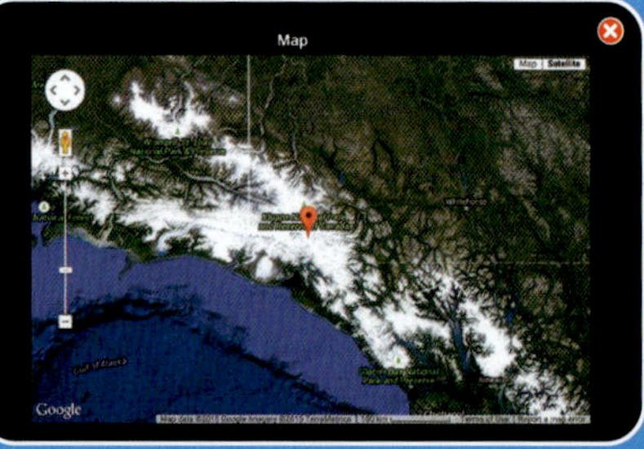

WEBLINKS

SLIDESHOWS

QUIZZES

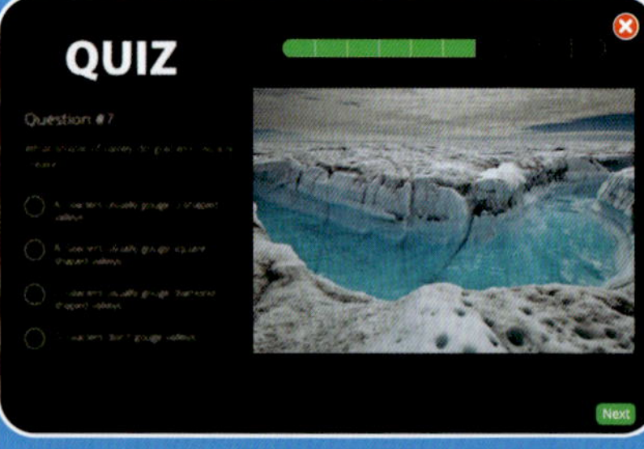

OPTIMIZED FOR

- ✓ TABLETS
- ✓ SMART BOARDS
- ✓ COMPUTERS
- ✓ AND MUCH MORE!

Published by Lightbox Learning Inc.
276 5th Avenue, Suite 704 #917
New York, NY 10001
Website: www.openlightbox.com

Project Coordinator Heather Kissock
Designer Terry Paulhus

Library of Congress Control Number: 2023939836

ISBN 978-1-5105-6684-2 (hardcover)
ISBN 978-1-5105-6685-9 (multi-user eBook)

Printed in Guangzhou, China
1 2 3 4 5 6 7 8 9 0 27 26 25 24 23

062023
111022

Photo Credits
Every reasonable effort has been made to trace ownership and to obtain permission to reprint copyright material. The publisher would be pleased to have any errors or omissions brought to its attention so that they may be corrected in subsequent printings. The publisher acknowledges Getty Images, Alamy, Bridgeman Images, Shutterstock, and Dreamstime as its primary image suppliers for this title.